MW01633222

Lessons from the Journey

Sherry McLaughlin

First Edition

ML Publishing, Warren, Michigan

Praise for Lessons from the Journey

"Wise beyond her years, Sherry's growth in spiritual courage and awareness has ascended to new heights in this engaging companion book to **Lessons from the Couch**.*"* –Anne Whitelaw

"'Journey' effortlessly addresses the basics of life, family & friends, self, work, money, and wraps it all up in a strong faith in God with a familiar perspective of everyday life that any one of us can relate to. The key lesson in this is knowing that with faith in God...ALL things are possible." –Rev. Laura Fluke

You tell the story of your journey with such clarity and humor. It is easy to become a part of what you share even if for a few minutes. Your trials, your faith, your acceptances are touching. Reading the recounting of your journey allows me to recount my own in the context of yours. It is soul sharing. Thanks for the gift. –Robert Teague, MD, Pulmonologist and Business Consultant

This book is a must have for all libraries. Even better than **Lessons from the Couch***, Sherry shares her heart and writes what others can't put into words. If you are an individual that has faith, but are not always sure how to use it, this book will empower you. Thank you for sharing your journey."* –Monique Robbins, Project Manager, Plexus Systems, LLC

*"***Journey** *sheds light onto the winding path that many of us are traveling. Sherry has the gift of eloquently verbalizing the everyday struggles that so many of us feel and can relate to. I applaud her efforts as she exposes her vulnerabilities and shares her very real and personal Christian experience. Each revelation and insight gained is a blessing to others on their own journey. And like* **Lessons from the Couch***, I just love the compilation of favorite inspirations at the end of the book!"*–Lou Ann Hummer, Merck, Inc.

"Each chapter exudes insight and wisdom into life's lessons, reminding the soul that it is not what happens to you . . . it is what you do with what happens to you!" –Carl Rundell, Salsa Dancer

"This book is about me. It describes my fear, exhaustion and lack of faith despite the amazing answers that God plops right in front of my dense self. Thank you for this wonderful reminder of His power, His love for me, and His ability to fix everything that I have screwed up...this book will be next to my bed and will constantly remind me of that until I am "grown up" in Him enough to really know it."–Lisa Jardine, Director of Campaigns and Special Projects, Andrews University

"Each journey's poignant lesson teaches and reminds us how to live, love and laugh—no matter where we are on the path."– Carol Lemieux, PTA, Wife and Mother Extraordinaire

"*A beautiful, spiritual journey for all of us whose lives seem overwhelming. Sherry's insight into her hopes and fears, and her trust and faith in God, are a true inspiration. This book is a blessing to all who are fortunate enough to read it.*"—Tonya Rivard, Type-A Sr. Account Executive, Spherion

"**Journey** *is an excellent sequel to* **Couch***! Your insightfulness is refreshing and enlightening. You've heard the phrase, 'Let go and let God?' Journey gives you examples of doing just that (and includes the results). You are blessed with a gift along with humble ability to have found a way to share it.* **Journey** *and* **Couch** *are refresher courses for those on the path, and great guidelines for those seeking the path. Blessings, light and love to you as you continue on your path. Thank you for sharing your love of life.* —Debra Moore, Reiki Master

Lessons from the Journey

Sherry McLaughlin

Published by:

ML Publishing
Warren, MI 48092, USA

Contents

About the Author

Sherry McLaughlin is the founder of the Michigan Institute for Human Performance, Inc. (MIHP) and TriPLAYnar Technology, Inc., headquartered in Southeastern Michigan. She is also married, a mother of a 12-year old autistic boy, a physical therapist, professional speaker and corporate consultant.

A 1990 graduate of Andrews University, Sherry has practiced in out-patient orthopedic rehabilitation clinics in Southeastern Michigan for over 15 years. She has also served as an adjunct faculty member for Macomb Community College since 1993, instructing courses in Musculoskeletal Physical Therapy and Kinesiology for the physical therapist assistant. She is an orthopedic certified specialist and a certified strength and conditioning specialist.

In 1998, she founded the Michigan Institute for Human Performance (MIHP), a consulting and training company specializing in injury prevention, sport-specific conditioning and orthopedic rehabilitation. She has developed several seminars including The Missing Link,

Optimal Athletic Conditioning, Hard Core Training, Optimal Golf and BackTalk, a back injury prevention program that is currently being utilized in several General Motors, Delphi, Sears and Northrop Grummon facilities in the United States. She has served as a consultant to USA Michigan Volleyball and the Detroit Vipers Hockey Organization. She is also the editor of *Synergy*, a bi-monthly newsletter of the MIHP Think Tank, which is currently circulated to health care and fitness professionals nationwide.

Sherry is known by her students, peers and seminar participants as a thought leader in biomechanics through her insightful methods in orthopedic rehabilitation, injury prevention and sports-specific conditioning. She is prolific in her ideas for innovative techniques and has captured them in workbooks, videos and articles that she produces to support her practice and teachings.

She has authored several manuals on biomechanics, musculoskeletal physical therapy and exercise prescription, as well as **Lessons from the Couch**.

She currently resides with her husband, son and two cousins in Birmingham, MI.

To Shelly—

Thank you for answering God's call and walking into my life.

My journey is undeniably better with you in it.

Journey on...

Preface

Most people look at me and think I have it all figured out. Family. Business. Life. But about the only thing I have figured out is that life is a journey—and if you choose to journey with God, you can bet things are going to get interesting.

I was perhaps born a natural journeyer. I've never been really great at standing still. Though I am content with the life I am living, my thoughts often wander into unchartered territory—and for better or worse, my feet sometimes follow. That can lead to meeting interesting people in interesting places. It can lead to standing on a mountaintop. It can also lead to the depths of despair.

The path of the journey is never straight. I know that now, better than I have at any other point in my life.

I think it is purposely a winding road, with lots of tight turns and twists, so that no matter how hard we crane our necks, it is impossible to see where we are going to end up. I suppose that's why they call it a walk of faith.

I once read that God never tells us where to go—He only asks that we follow Him. He never gets lost, so we can rest assured that if we follow, we will ultimately end up where we are supposed to be.

Once you realize that, then it really is all about the journey. The way I see it, you can choose the path of least resistance, the one that is paved, safe and very well-traveled. Or, you can step out in faith, blaze a new trail and climb a mountain. You might take a few spills and get a little bruised along the way, but I promise you, the scenery is much nicer.

I know. I'm apparently on that mountain path—and that is what this book is about. The season of my journey where I climbed higher than I've ever climbed, fallen harder than I've ever fallen, met some of the best people I will ever meet and learned what it was like to walk with God.

It has been the best of times and the worst of times—and I wouldn't trade a minute of it for the world. I hope to perhaps meet you on my path, but if I don't, rest assured—I'll see you on the other side of the mountain.

Here are the lessons I've learned…

Sherry McLaughlin

Birmingham, Michigan

2005

Chapter 1

Hero

"Explore your mind, discover yourself,
then give the best that is in you to your age and to your world.
There are heroic possibilities
waiting to be discovered in every person."
–Wilfred A. Peterson

Have you ever run into someone that seemed bigger than life? Someone who everything they touched seemed to turn to gold? Someone who's every word you would remember? Every time you pictured them, they were doing something great. Something large. Something significant. If you ever got to meet that person, or if they ever sent you an email or had a conversation with you—you stood at the top of the world for just a moment.

Everybody needs a hero.

"I learned so many things about life from taking your class," a former student recently told me. It had been 7 years since she sat in my classroom. "Remember the story about the 10-second kiss?" she continued. I grinned in amusement. I vaguely remember the details of the story. In fact, such stories were thrown into the middle of my lectures to combat the glassy-eyed looks of overwhelmed students. When the brains looked like they were on overload, I usually jumped into story mode about something totally unrelated to kinesiology or orthopedics. Something related to life. Evidently, they contained some timeless lessons. "It changed my life." She said.

Now, you are all probably wondering about the 10-second kiss. That story actually belongs in another book. It is, however, self-explanatory. Give it a try and you will probably have a story to tell yourself. But, I digress.

Here is the point. It became apparent to me on that occasion, and several times in the recent past, that I was that person to some. A hero. My position as a teacher and lecturer lends itself to that, I think. I mean, here I am standing in front of a group of people who have paid to hear what I have to say. Many of the things I will teach are foreign to them. They have very little basis to launch an argument against what I say. They are in the position to soak things up and soak it up well, because in the end they will be given a test. And how they do on that test, on that particular day, will determine the course of their future. Pretty high stakes, huh?

It should make those in positions of authority take pause. Being someone's hero is a huge undertaking because it is likely that you will run into some of your admirers down the road—and they never forget what you say.

Just for the record, I get up in the morning and put my pants on one leg at a time. I don't always eat healthy and I get grouchy like everyone else. Just ask my husband. Sometimes I can't figure out what to wear and I certainly don't press my cape…um…I mean my shirt every morning before I head off to work. I've got even bigger news for you.

Even heroes need a hero.

When I first met my life coach, she didn't appear bigger than life. She is younger than me. But she sits in this beautiful office and every week when we touch base, I sit across from her and we talk. Maybe a better description would be that I blurt out my cares and woes, and she listens and gently guides my life back into perspective.

For those of you that know the kind of life I lead, that is no minor task. My days are long and the nights are short. I often have a list of things to accomplish in a day that probably should be spread over a week. I have a lot of people to answer to and answer for. One of my favorite things to blurt out in the middle of a hectic day is, "Stop the bus! I'm getting off!"

So, there my coach sits, week after week. She doesn't say much, but in the stillness of her office, I listen and I learn. I learn about faith and trust. Hope and love. I learn that sometimes the hard things to do are the ones you want to run towards. And I remember every word.

I remember it because it is life-changing.

"You have this uncanny way of recalling every conversation we have," she once said to me. You would too, I thought, if you only really understood how much this time means to me.

Before I knew it, I had a hero. I found myself wondering what she was like outside of the office. It was tough for me to picture her doing anything but sitting in a chair spouting words of wisdom. Rest assured she irons her cape…I mean clothes…before she comes to work in the morning—I've seen it. But I found myself wondering about other things. What does she like to eat? Does she have any hobbies? What does she like to talk about when someone isn't paying her? I found my curiosity mounting and I was a bit frustrated by this. Why did I even care?

In the latest Spiderman movie, there was a scene where Spiderman was battling a villain on a high-speed train. The passengers in the train were frightened, but at the same time knew there was hope because their hero was in the mix. After a long battle, it appeared Spiderman had been defeated. Lying on the train floor, a crowd formed around him only to realize his mask had been ripped off.

"He's just a boy," they said in shock. His secret had been revealed and in that moment their view of him changed. But not in the way one would expect. Instead of being disappointed, their spirits seemed to be lifted. They helped their hero up, gave him the look that said, "your secret is safe with us" and with that, he was back in the battle.

When someone seems bigger than life, it somehow gives us hope for a better tomorrow. And when we find out our heroes are human, it gives us hope that we can make a better tomorrow. I think God knew that when He chose to become a man. After all, when it boils down to it, that is what a hero is—a normal person doing something significant—being who they were designed to be and changing the world by living their God-given purpose. Super-human heroes.

And now I've got even bigger news for you.

No matter how insignificant you feel, there is probably someone in your life that looks at you with awe. Someone who hangs on to what you say. Someone who wishes they could be just like you. They might be young or old. You might meet them early in life or later. You don't get to choose when you will add it to your resume'. But it is a fact of life—and if we all could realize it, this world would be a better place.

"One person can and does make a difference.
In everyone's life, at some time, our inner fire goes out.
It is then burst into flame by an encounter
with another human being."
—Albert Schweitzer

Everybody is a hero. Live accordingly.

Journey Tip #1

Everybody needs a hero.

Even heroes need a hero.

Super heroes are great.

Super-*human* heroes are even better.

Everyone is a hero.

Live and speak accordingly.

Chapter 2

Rewind

"Mistakes are lessons of wisdom. The past cannot be changed.
The future is yet in your power."
–Hugh White

You always hurt the ones you love. That's what they say, isn't it? I'm just wondering how "they" got to know me so well.

It was the day of my husband's birthday. Oh, how

I wish that was all that particular day had in store for me. But in the typical fashion of my life, his birthday happened to fall on the same day that I had 15 patients scheduled before noon, a staff intervention I needed to take care of and suitcases that needed to be packed so that we could leave for our family vacation before three o'clock. Before we left town, I had to make sure to send off a document that had been due the week before and pay some bills so that I could spend money without guilt. Pure insanity.

Knowing I had already failed to have something ready for him in the morning, I managed to greet him "Happy Birthday" and comment on how well he was aging. I really meant it. But in the back of my mind, I figured that would buy me some time until I could get to the store and pick up a gift and a card. I would do it on the way home from the office.

You know what they say about the best laid plans of mice and men. They were right again.

My morning flew by and before I knew it, I was hustling to get home, meet my deadline and pack up the family SUV. The boys were getting antsy to get out of town and I was holding them up.

I hastily threw everything into the back seat and settled in for the 3-hour ride to our destination. As I sat in the back seat, (my son had commandeered the passenger front seat), it dawned on me that there was no way I was going to be able to make an escape to buy the anticipated card and present. I reached into my briefcase, recalling that I had purchased a card awhile back that I had never used. Perfect. I could write out the card while we traveled and present it to him when we arrived. He would never know the difference.

I dug deep into the pockets of my briefcase and retrieved the card. It looked like it had been bought a year ago. Dog-eared on one corner and bent into a slight curve, I dusted it off. It would have to do. Smoothing out the wrinkles, I glanced at the picture on the front, opened it up and began to write. As I penned words of love and deep meaning, my eyes kept wandering to the message printed on the right hand side. It read:

Birthdays…a great time to get down with your bad self.

Clearly, I must have bought it when I was in a slightly more humorous mood. Who was I kidding? He was not going to be fooled into thinking that I had actually chosen this card for him. Ugh.

I ripped up the card and threw it back into my briefcase. Oh, well. Maybe he won't care. I mean, after all, he is a grown man. They aren't supposed to care about this sentimental stuff anyway, are they? I rationalized my error away. Nothing I could do now. There was always next year.

Be careful what you ask for. That's another thing they say, isn't it? If there was one thing I had insisted on when we got married, it was that we would always be honest with each other. Eight days later, my need for honesty slapped me in the face.

"I just want you to know that it really hurt my feelings that you didn't do anything special for my birthday," he said. "It sounds crazy, but it's true. I know you were tired and busy and I feel silly even bringing it up now. I just wanted you to know."

Hearing that was like a knife in my heart. My gut reaction was to immediately launch into a dissertation about my busy schedule and place the blame on being rushed out of town. But, sometimes the Lord blesses us by sealing our mouths shut. Thank God He did it on that day.

I thanked my husband for his honesty and sat

speechless before my error. I had allowed business, deadlines and the busyness of my life to oust my soulmate from the #1 spot on my priority list.

We often hurt the ones we love because we figure they will understand. But even if they do, is hurting them really what we want?

I knew I had to fix this—and it couldn't wait a year. I couldn't change the past, but I still had control of the future. I put my creative hat on and set out to put my plan in place.

The next morning, my husband awoke to a surprise package on the kitchen table. As he peered inside, he pulled out a card I had chosen just for him. He sat down and read:

As I sit here in the stillness of this house, I know how lucky I am. You are the kind of husband so many women hope for—and I am yours.

I love you so deeply—I really do.

So, please forgive me for being too tired or too frustrated or too whatever to let you know that—especially when it really counts. And forgive me for not being perceptive enough to see how you are hurting at times. It has been a rough year, but I wouldn't give up a minute of it for the lessons that I've learned about life and love—and you.

I am honored that you trusted me enough to tell me how you really felt about your birthday. I honestly didn't realize how much it meant to you, and I'm embarrassed to say that. Because it IS your special day—a day that, frankly, I'm thrilled happened. In being too busy and too tired, I failed to really celebrate a day that is equally important to me.

I love you and I love you in my life and that is reason to celebrate.

So in typical "straight-A Shei" fashion, I have decided to remedy my faux pas and declare today your offical:
39th REWIND Birthday!
A time to celebrate you and who you are to me—
A time to be thankful for a chance to fix what I royally screwed up…

Oh, and date night dinner is on me!

Love,
Shei

"Happy birthday," I said, as I came around the corner.

"You have no idea how much this means to me," he replied as he pulled me close. The tears in his eyes and the gentle kiss he planted on my forehead said it all.

It turned out to be one of the best birthdays we have ever celebrated together. And it had all the makings of a great story. Love, error, forgiveness and a second chance.

Better late than never. That's what they say. And they were right again. Few mistakes are ever fatal—unless you allow them to be.

Nobody is perfect. You are only human, after all. Admitting it is the first step. The next time you royally mess something up, thank God for the ones you love and for the lessons life teaches.

Then rewind—and try it again.

Journey Tip #2

Mistakes are seldom fatal—

Unless you allow them to be.

Nobody is perfect.

If you royally mess up,

exercise your power to

REWIND

and give it another try.

Chapter 3

Mutual Save

"…And if you find a love that's tender,
if you find someone who's true, thank the Lord.
He's been doubly good to you."
—Amy Grant

Let me tell you a story about a wedding.

From the surface, it looked like most other weddings. Held in a church, the day carried all of the human drama that a wedding day usually holds. A nervous groom. Groomsmen trying to figure out the intricacies of a tuxedo. The heavy anticipation of the bride's arrival and the crazy, busy wedding coordinator orchestrating the moves of everyone from the guests signing the book, to the bridal party, to the people responsible for documenting the event on film. Organized chaos.

I know, I was there. I was one of the photographers.

Photographing weddings is not necessarily one of my favorite things to do. In fact, it is downright nerve-wracking for me. It is one of the least forgiving events in that if you mess something up, it would be nearly impossible to do a re-take. I mean, can you imagine? "Cut! Um, sorry guys, I sort of missed that first kiss thing, can you back up and try it again?" No rewinds. No do-overs—and that makes me nervous. Also, I am such a sucker for a good love story that when the ceremony gets good, the view through my lens somehow gets fuzzy. Thank God for auto focus.

That being said, it is a privilege to be placed in charge of cementing into history one of the biggest days of a lifetime and I was grateful to be part of it.

The bride arrived in the back of a chauffeured '57 Chevy limousine. As I stood outside of the vehicle, poised to get a shot, the window rolled down and she motioned me over.

"I want you to know how much it means to me that you are a part of this," she said.

"I am honored that I was asked to be here," I replied as I squeezed her shoulder. "You look stunning."

"Thanks. I'm going crazy in here."

"As it should be," I added with a grin on my face.

Eventually, the guests were all seated. The bridesmaids lined up and the processional began.

Their story was part of the ceremony. Boy calls girl. Girl doesn't return phone call. Boy calls girl again. Girl finally returns phone call to conduct a 1-hour interview prior to meeting the boy. He obviously passed the test.

It was a whirlwind romance by today's standards. In less than a year, they met, fell in love and were now standing at the altar. Each of them had prayed on separate occasions that God would lead them to their life mate and this moment was a testament to answered prayers.

Prior to this event, I knew very little about the

couple. I was asked to do the job at the last minute. But as I milled about the crowd that day, their story unfolded.

It's sort of funny how people feel compelled to talk to the photographer. At least they felt like it on that day. I got to hear stories from her college days when life was crazy and carefree and weekends were filled with interesting social engagements. I got to hear from a young girl about how the bride had taught her how to figure skate. She even showed me some moves right there at the table. And I sat next to a couple that told me his story and replayed the details of their engagement.

"I've never seen him so taken by a girl!" The man sitting next to me explained. He and the groom had been friends since high school. Class of '82. He was an excavator and the groom owned a trucking company that delivered gravel. "I dig the ditches and he brings stuff to put in the holes," he described with his small town accent. "His first marriage ended in divorce. It was really rough on him," he continued. "His son was the best thing to come out of the marriage. When he finally decided to start dating again I remember him calling me after every date to say, 'No, she's not the one.'"

Then one day, he received a call of a different tone. He described the Herculean effort put into making the night of the proposal absolutely perfect. As he watched his friend perform a minor landscape makeover, he remembers looking at him and saying, "Man, this girl's got ya good!"

To many of the people who witnessed this fine occasion, it was obvious that she had saved his life. He revealed this much, with tears in his eyes choking back the emotion when he said, "You are my answer to prayer." He now had a wife and his son had a mother. The journey for him had been difficult and painful. He had searched and searched and waited a long time.

But that's not the whole story. At least, not the way I saw it.

As my lens focused on the couple time and time again, during their first dance, sitting at the head table, or in the moments when they thought nobody was watching, I caught a certain expression or a touch—subtle moments where she looked at him with the admiration and the depth that can only come from someone who felt exactly the same way.

To most observers, she had saved him. But to the keen observer, and to this photographer, it was clear that she, too, had been rescued.

A mutual save.

And that's what makes this one feel like it is going to last forever. Because when things get rough, as they will in a marriage, people will tend to run towards their rescuer. To the haven that God granted the two of them in each other. Safe. Solid. Strong.

That's how you know when you have fallen in love for the right reason. Not because things are always a bed of roses. But because when things happen that should make you run, you choose to run towards him—and not away. A choice, not an obligation. It is perhaps one of the greatest mysteries of a good love story.

Trust me. I know.

Journey Tip #3

Real love involves a mutual save—
a shared feeling of gratitude for the safety
each person finds in the other.

Real love feels like a choice, not an
obligation—especially when things go wrong.

Chapter 4

Give me a sign

Give me a sign of your goodness...
for you, O LORD, have helped me and comforted me.
—Psalm 86:17

Ever have one of those days where fear and dread overtake you? I never did—until I started my own business. I wasn't one of those people born with the entrepreneurial bug. Quite the contrary, I was the perfect employee. Showed up on time, did my best work for 8 hours, made sure my paperwork was caught up and then left work—physically and mentally. I had time to stop at the gym and work out, pick up some groceries on the way home and get dinner on the table for the family. My life was ordered, predictable and virtually stress-free.

I had so much extra time on my hands that I was able to pick up a teaching job and start little businesses on the side. I started an outdoor photography business, then a seminar and consulting business. I even did some freelance graphic design work. People told me I had quite the entrepreneurial spirit, but it really doesn't count when you can still bank on a paycheck from your full-time job with benefits.

"I don't understand why you keep dabbling your toe in the water," my husband would say. "You need to just jump right in." He had owned and operated his own business since he was 23 and couldn't understand why I didn't want to join him in the insanity.

Then, one day, the bug bit me.

I opened my first private practice in the Fall of 2002. I had visions of grandeur that I would open my doors and people would be rushing through. Those first few months when we were all sitting around waiting for a patient to come through the doors were some of my toughest. My line of credit dwindled quickly and even after our caseload picked up, a major insurance carrier failed to cut us our first check for 5-months. I was working a 50-hour workweek and still trying to catch up on things at home. Things were feeling bleak.

In about a year, things started turning around. I started actually being able to pay myself. I reduced my work hours and I set out on getting my life back. Then, the unthinkable happened.

"Are you interested in expanding your practice?" an investor asked.

"Absolutely not." I said.

I had been approached before about expansion opportunities and had answered the same way every time. You know how they tell you that you forget the pains of childbirth once the baby is born? Well, I have news for you. My son is 12 and I can still remember it. Not much different when starting up a business.

This investor, however, was a bit more persistent. His inquiry launched a series of discussions and a whole lot of prayer on my end that ultimately led to the opening of MIHP West—my 2nd private practice.

Despite my best efforts, things did not go smoothly. After a 9-month delay in the expansion project, mounting up debt faster than I could blink, I found myself questioning the Lord, again.

Now, I am not usually one to be so bold as to ask God for a sign. I mean, who am I to demand an explanation from the Lord of the Universe? He had taken care of me thus far, why couldn't I just believe?

It's funny how we can read about the Israelites in the Bible and laugh at their doubt. I mean, if I had witnessed the parting of the Red Sea and seen water come from a rock and watched food fall from the sky all as signs that God was with me, my faith would not have wavered. Or would it have? Am I really any better than they were?

I couldn't shake the feeling of fear and dread one morning. So, I boldly prayed to the Lord, "I know you have led me to this point for a reason. And forgive my doubt now. But I need to know if I'm in the right place—if I've heard You right. Because this doesn't feel right. I need a sign, and if you could make it really clear, that would be great. I'm a little too exhausted to be that perceptive." And with that, I headed out the door to the office.

Once immersed in patient care, my mind wandered away from the worry of business. That day, I received a dozen roses from a patient in the morning, a dozen roses from another patient in the afternoon, both accompanied with cards affirming the value of our service.

You have changed my life, one individual wrote.

Thank you for the sacrifices you make to do things differently, another stated.

Later in the day as I was sitting at my desk mulling over bills, my office manager stepped into my office. I must have looked worried.

"Are you OK?" she asked.

"Yeah," I muttered. I had asked for a sign—and received two, and yet my worry continued.

"Here's your mail," she said.

Amidst the letters was a card from a former patient. Eloquently written and covered with ink from front to back, it read:

God surely works all things together for good. I would not have met you unless I sprained my ankle…Thank you for all you have done for me!

Could the signs have been any clearer? It is both awe-inspiring and sometimes a bit frightening that God would hear and answer so quickly and so clearly.

Later on that day, I glanced out the window and saw that I had a flat tire. Great. Just what I needed. It was 97° outside, I had a bunch of patients to treat and I certainly didn't have any extra money to hire someone to change it. The Israelite in me was rearing its ugly head. I meandered out to the gym and mentioned it to one of my staff members.

A patient overheard and said, "Don't worry, Sherry, I'll change it for you."

Slightly embarrassed, I replied, "You will do no such thing. I'll get it taken care of." After all, how could I let a back patient go out and change my tire? Hardly a good marketing campaign.

I proceeded with my work of the day. Unbeknownst to me, that gentlemen secured my keys and set about the task of changing the tire. I saw him come back into the building, covered in gravel and sweating. "It's all done!" he said.

"You are an answer to prayer," I replied—and I meant it.

Give me a sign and make it clear, I had asked the Lord of the Universe. I don't know how much clearer He could have been. I asked for one. He sent me four. And in the course of a day, amidst those signs it was as if He was saying, "You are on the right track and I am taking care of you."

I feel a little silly now. I know that if I had to cross the Red Sea, God probably would have parted it for me that day. Thank God I worship a God of patience. One who forgives the fact that I sometimes lose site of the big picture and fail to see the big miracles He works in my life.

One who realizes that sometimes all I really need is a pat on the back…and someone to come and change my tire.

Journey Tip #4

If you ask God for a sign,
He cares enough to answer.

Make sure you care enough to notice—
and remember it.

Chapter 5

The Money Thing

"Who of you by worrying can add a single hour to his life?
...But seek first his kingdom and his righteousness."
–Matthew 6:27, 33 (NIV)

"You are a perfectionist and a control freak," she said. Wow. That was a powerful statement. If there is one thing that can be said about a good life coach it is that they don't pull any punches. Unfortunately, I think my coach graduated with high honors.

I had just finished detailing out the worries of my week. Bills, payroll and the surmounting stress that is associated with the fact that families would starve if I didn't come up with enough money by the end of the week. A mentor once told me, "There is nothing like the gut-wrenching feeling you get when payday is Friday and you don't have enough money in the bank—that feeling will develop character." He was right. I felt like I had an elephant in my stomach—and it was doing cartwheels.

"Have you ever missed a payroll?" she asked.

"Umm…no," I replied. Not yet, anyway.

"Let me tell you a story," she said. "Let's just say payday is Friday. You get up Monday morning and pray, 'Lord, please help me to make payroll.' Then you head out the door and begin to try to make it happen. You make a few phone calls, check your books, ask your secretary how much money came in, etc., etc. You worry about it all day and at the end of the day, you are still short. So, on Tuesday morning, you do the same thing. You get up, say a prayer and then go about your business of trying to make it happen. And at the end of that day, you still don't have the money. Does this sound about right?"

I nodded in agreement. That is exactly how my weeks would go.

"So, just imagine that God is holding this bag of money in His hand and He is looking down at you saying, 'Trust me, Sherry. Give it to Me.' And He is watching you busily running around, worrying and stressed-out despite the fact that you had asked for His help in the morning."

What was the point, I wondered.

"So finally, you get to Thursday night. You have exhausted your resources. Payday is the next day and you have still come up short. At that point, you flop down on the floor, look up to God and say, 'OK, I can't do it anymore. I don't know where else to turn or what else to do. If it is Your will that I make payroll, then You are going to have to make it happen.'"

She paused.

"And it is at that moment, that God drops the bag of money in your lap." She let that statement sink in and then added, "Now, wouldn't it be easier to just give it to Him on Monday?"

The wisdom in her story sunk in. She was right again. Who did I think I was fooling by asking God for help and then trying to find back-up—just in case? In case of what? The notion was laughable, really. My day was hectic because I was trying to take care of my stuff and everybody else's—I was even trying to manage the Lord of the Universe.

Hire the best and then let them shine. This was a mantra I had stuck to since I opened my business and it had worked splendidly. In picking my staff wisely, I was able to step back and just watch the beauty of their work unfold. They were intelligent, effective and efficient and I had to do very little to motivate them. I actually enjoyed watching them work. They were all sitting in the right seat on the bus, so to speak, being able to capitalize on their strengths and experience success daily. It was the one thing I was most proud of in my business—the one area where I truly felt successful.

Trust in the Lord with all thine heart;
and lean not unto thine own understanding.
In all thy ways acknowledge Him
and He shall direct thy paths.
—Proverbs 3:5,6 (NIV)

I'm not one to rave about miracles—sometimes I think I'm too sensible for my own good. But I do have a story of my own now. Since the day my coach challenged me with really giving the payroll issue to God, I have continued to meet every payroll—with a lot less worry and sometimes a week ahead of time.

It's a lesson for the ages. Hire God. Put Him in the driver's seat. Delegate. And then get out of His way.

Journey Tip #5

When asking God for help,
sometimes the answer only comes
after we get out of His way.

We should ask and believe.
That's it.
God doesn't require back-up.

Chapter 6

Marathon

"He who waits upon the Lord shall renew their strength...
they will walk and not be weary, they shall run and not be faint."
—Isaiah 40:31 (NIV)

"So, what's going on with you today?" she asked, as I sat across from her on the couch. It had been over 5 months since I'd first met her. I felt a lump rise in my throat.

"I'm just exhausted," I replied. Looking away, I realized this was going to be one tough session. The business expansion had taken its toll. I had increased my workload, putting in 12-hour days and was trying to juggle the finances to stay afloat. "It is the weirdest thing," I continued. "I imagine this line and to the left of it is what I picture to be a normal life. To the right of it is insanity. Last week, I felt like I was way over to the left, but I stepped into a situation last week that reminded me just how close to the right I sometimes feel." I went on to explain how transparent I felt—even local store owners had begun to inquire if anything was wrong.

"What did you say when they asked?" she said.

"I put on my happy face and told them things were great."

"That's why you are exhausted, Sherry."

I looked up at her as she continued. "You are so busy trying to put up a façade of what you think people want to see. How about being real? Let's just cut to the chase and stop the charade. I have worked with you long enough. I know you well enough."

I do believe she is trying to make me cry, I thought.

Not going to happen. Going to pull it together. I WILL not lose it. "But isn't there a time when full disclosure is inappropriate?" I argued. "I mean, so someone asks me how I'm doing and I'm just supposed to answer, 'My life sucks. Thanks for asking.' Isn't there ever a time not to be real?" I asked.

"You could simply answer 'I'm not doing really well today.' At the very least, you might get some encouragement."

Great. Not only do I feel like a failure in business… now I can't even do this right. The perfectionist in me was rearing its ugly head. Tears were welling up.

"You are on the brink. Don't fight this emotion. Let it happen," she said.

That was it. In a matter of seconds I was reduced to tears. How on earth did I get to this point? Why did I work so hard and still feel like a failure? The exhaustion had finally overwhelmed me—and in the safety of my coach's office, I lost it. Not one of my proudest moments. In fact, I had never felt weaker.

"The tissues are no extra charge," she said as she placed a box beside me. "You don't need to explain it right now. It doesn't even have to make sense. Just let it be. This is a gift, Sherry." And with that, she opened her Bible and began to read Psalms 91.

Life occasionally hands you defining moments and for me, this was one of them. There in the safety of her office, feeling extremely vulnerable, I heard the words I had read before—only this time they meant so much more.

"He who dwells in the shelter of the Most High, will rest in the shadow of the Almighty," she read. "…Because he loves me, says the Lord, I will rescue him…I will be with him in trouble, I will deliver him and honor him," she continued. Even as the tears flowed, I felt a sense of calm and relief. The pressure cooker had been uncorked. We spent several minutes in silence.

"What happens at the end of a marathon?" she asked. "You work with those runners. You've been to the races. What happens after they cross the finish line?"

"Umm…they put their arms up in the air as a sign of victory."

"Do they all come across the finish line smiling?" she continued.

"Not all of them. Some of them collapse." I answered, images of a specific race appearing in my head.

"And do they just lay there for a couple of hours—all alone?" she pressed on.

"No. Someone comes to help them. They get oxygen and an I.V. and some medical attention."

"Hmm…so when they are the most exhausted, they are not left alone. They are given nutrition and air—the basics and someone comes to the rescue," she reflected.

Her point was becoming clear and she gave it time to sink in. In all of the months I had spent meeting with her, this was probably the least we had talked. In my exhaustion and defeat, I found myself unable to form even a complete sentence. Just when I thought I had it pulled together, the tears would begin to flow again.

This is a gift. I just kept hearing her voice in my head. "I just really hope I'm doing the right thing," I said. "I've prayed about this the whole time. I've done my best to give it to God—to not worry. I just wish if I was meant to fail, He would just tell me. If I'm supposed to succeed, then it would be good to know that, too."

"Ah, so you can control it all over again," she

answered with a hint of sarcasm. I gave her a weak smile. "You've followed what God has told you to do this far," she continued. "He hasn't let you down yet. When He wants you to act on something, He'll let you know. Until then, just sit tight and wait for further instruction."

In this fast-paced world, sitting tight isn't often an option. In order to compete, you feel like you have to keep moving. "Sometimes when our insides are moving so fast, when we are the most worried and the most confused, that's when we make ourselves crazy busy. It's almost as if we are moving fast on the outside, because at least that way, our insides and outsides match. We run on 'turbo speed' for so long, it's no wonder we get exhausted," she explained. "If you stop for a moment, I promise you, the world will not collapse."

I felt like I was at the end of a marathon. Exhausted. Hurting. On the brink of collapse. And there was my coach—right where she was supposed to be—to remind me to take shelter, rest and wait on the Lord.

An hour later, I wasn't any richer. My situation hadn't really changed. But I felt like a new woman. Perspective is everything.

Life is a marathon. Run hard. Rest safely. Gather your strength. And run again. The chance to run is one of life's greatest gifts. The chance to be picked up when you fall…is the other.

Journey Tip #6

Life is a marathon.

God never said you wouldn't get tired.

But He did say you would never run alone.

Chapter 7

The Center of the Universe

"Sing for joy, O heavens, for the LORD has done this;
shout aloud, O earth beneath. Burst into song, you mountains,
you forests and all your trees..."
—Isaiah 44:23 (NIV)

Welcome to Concrete, WA—the Center of the Known Universe. That was the inscription on a wooden sign on the side of Highway 20 in Northern Washington. A town where time appears to stand still—where God's creation screams louder than man's. Set in the foothills of the Cascade Mountains, Concrete is the kind of town that is still asleep at 9 a.m. on a Sunday morning. It is the kind of town where the City Center sign points in only two directions—go left for auto parts and churches and go right for a restaurant, supply store and City Hall. It is the kind of town where the streets are simply named A, B, C, D and E Ave. Though hardly anybody lives here, it is the kind of place that everybody should—even for just a short period of time—at least once in their life.

When your mind is racing to keep up with your schedule and your thoughts are being drowned out by cell phones, pagers and PDA's—when you are moving so fast you don't have time to feel, in the simplicity of a quiet town like Concrete, WA, it is easy for God to speak to your soul. Or maybe, I should say, it is a lot easier to hear His voice.

I know. I was there once.

Not initially by choice. I had received an invitation to the wedding of a friend. Being from the Midwest. I had all intentions of just sending a card and a gift. But at the last minute, she asked me to be in it. Me?! I was easily 10 years older than her and the other girls. I valued her friendship, more than she probably will ever know, but we hadn't really spent that much time together.

"I know its last minute," she said, "but I've really been thinking about it and I just really want you to be a part of it."

In my shock, I accepted. I would work out the details later. Bridesmaids dress. Plane ticket. Babysitter. Rental car. Hotel. Patient re-scheduling. My mind was spinning with the items added to my to-do list.

I planned on making a vacation of it. After all, it had been years since my husband and I had gotten away, and the pressures of business ownership were weighing heavy at the moment.

"Wanna head out West with me?" I asked.

He looked at me longingly and said, "I really don't think I can." In one fell swoop, my visions of a 6-day vacation wilted to a 3-day getaway—solo.

I left town immediately after seeing my last patient on Friday. I was scheduled to arrive in Seattle at 1:00 a.m. Saturday. Settling into my plane seat, I didn't feel much like talking, but the 15-year old boy sitting next to me sure did.

"Do you fly a lot?" he asked.

"Depends on the time of year," I replied.

"Hmm…want a piece of gum?

"Sure."

And with that, the conversation was on its way in the style that only an adventurous teenage boy could take it. Topics ranged from being on the swim team to playing golf to being in a band. The conversation rose to a crescendo when he pulled out a magazine and held it up for me to see.

"This is what I'm going to buy one day," he said with a gleam in his eye. My gaze fell on a picture of a chopper—bright orange with yellow trim. He began to fill me in on the bike's specifications. I didn't understand a word—but I recognized his excitement.

I used to feel that way about dreams.

He went silent for a few minutes as he flipped through the pages of the magazine. I turned on my iPod, closed my eyes and tried to let the music erase the stress of my work week.

I felt a tap on my shoulder. Opening one eye, my gaze fell on his awkward, but eager, grin.

"So, what kind of music do you have on there…"

I chuckled, "You'd hate it."

"Do you have any Van Halen?

"Nah. Mostly relaxing stuff. Piano music. That kind of thing."

"What radio stations do you listen to?"

I had to laugh. Clearly, the conversation was on again. I turned off my iPod, rolled up the headphones and turned towards him. Evidently, he had not taken *Social Cues 101* yet and I didn't have the heart to shoot him down. Bring on the talk.

And bring it he did. I learned about his family and what his dad did for a living. He described his latest wipe out on his bike and showed me the scars. He told me he played the trombone—the very instrument I played in high school and college. Animated. Energetic. Excited.

Before I knew it, the plane was preparing to land. He offered me a final piece of gum, taking a guess at how many hundreds of pieces he must have chewed in his lifetime. Spearmint was his favorite.

"Hope I didn't talk your ear off," he said. You did, I thought. But it was good for my soul.

I'll never forget his face—bright, eager eyes behind large, plastic-rimmed glasses. He stood 6 feet tall on big, awkward feet. And he had a smile that could light up a room. You could tell that, at least for the moment, all was well in his world—so well that he just had to share it.

I hopped on a connector flight from Phoenix to Seattle, settling into my aisle seat. I caught a few minutes of sleep only to open my eyes and see a gentleman from across the aisle smiling at me.

Oh, no, I thought. Here we go again.

"Where are you coming from?" he inquired.

I answered and the conversation grew wings. Some would say that I'm crazy for not just shutting these people down, but I'm a firm believer in the fact that God sends people our way for a reason. Once again, my curiosity got the best of me.

Turns out he was a budding entrepreneur, flying to Seattle to check out a product that would decrease the slipperiness of a wet floor. I could appreciate his excitement in the possibilities of a new venture. I used to feel that way once. It's the kind of mindset that is necessary to take that leap of faith.

Faith. The substance of things hoped for and the evidence of things not seen.

When an idea forms in your mind—when you can see it happening—that's when great things can happen. You are dreaming and you have momentum—the kind that sees possibilities and is yet untouched by failure.

The mark of a visionary is just that—to be able to maintain a vision of where you want to be despite the obstacles that jump up. People have called me a visionary. Right now, I was feeling like someone had put Vaseline on my lenses.

"So, what do you do for a living?" he asked.

I chuckled. Do you have a week to listen? I thought. "I'm a physical therapist," I said. It was my attempt to be minimalist and he would have none of that.

"What do you know about treating rotator cuff tears?" he asked. "I'm a physician's assistant for a large orthopedic practice in Palm Springs."

The geek in me was fighting to come out. I was doing my best to squelch it.

"We see a lot of people after surgery who get tendonitis during rehab," he continued. "Do you have any idea why? We can't figure it out?"

That was the kicker. I launched into a dissertation of the biomechanics of arm elevation and its connections to the spine, hips and ankles. I heard myself telling him about the work our practice had done in pioneering an assessment tool that allowed us to make these connections and come up with viable solutions. We discussed surgical procedures and treatment options for the next hour, going back and forth excitedly like two kids. The conversation culminated in an exchange of contact information and a possible invitation to do a seminar in Palm Springs.

"I like your passion," he said.

I liked feeling it again, I thought.

Two long flights. Two conversations. Two reminders of what life can feel like when you step out in faith and allow yourself to feel the excitement in possibilities and simple things again.

Chance encounters? I smiled. Probably not.

After catching a few hours of sleep at the hotel, I spent the morning in downtown Seattle, taking in the sights and smells of Pike Place Market, photographing the locals and grazing on the fresh fruits and vegetables. The calm waters of Elliot Bay set in the backdrop of skyscrapers and shipping yards was a picture of nature and industry colliding.

I made my way to Discovery Park, Seattle's version of Central Park. Following the trail system through various lookouts and forests, I landed on the sands of the Puget Sound. I took my shoes off and felt the sand beneath my feet. A warm breeze blew across the water. I strolled along the water until I found a spot to sit—away from the city and the kids playing.

It was there that I felt God touch my soul. As I looked across the water and watched the sailboats glide by, I prayed that the frenzy of my heart would disappear. I asked God to reveal His will in my life and to speak to me—here in this quiet place, where the obligations of work and home were so far removed. I was at a point in my life where I needed answers.

I looked up just as the clouds parted to reveal the shadow of the Olympic mountain range. I didn't hear a voice, but I was reminded of His greatness and that the faith of a mustard seed could move those glorious structures.

I could stay here forever, I thought, almost forgetting the purpose of my trip. I had a wedding to attend. The bride was expecting me this evening and I was still two hours away from my final destination. Better get a move on.

I delayed as long as possible, not feeling much like socializing. But I felt an urging to get on the road, so I hiked through wooded trails back to my car, thankful for the few hours of solitude I had gotten.

As I headed north on Interstate 5, the scenery changed from the cityscape to the lush green of the foothills of the Cascades. I drove along the Skajit River—a skyline of mountain ranges before me. It was as if God was saying, "You thought the Puget Sound was great—let me show you more of what I've done."

I worked my way to Highway 20, where the roads began to wind in and around the mountains. By the time I pulled into Concrete, I felt like a different person—or maybe more like the person I used to be.

I navigated my way to my friend's house. Cows and horses grazed in the neighboring fields. I pulled up into the driveway of a house that was decorated for a wedding. Hanging baskets lined the wrap-around porch. I walked into the sounds of laughter and conversation. My friend jumped up to greet me with a hug.

"Thank you so much for coming!"

It had been several weeks since I had seen her. She gave me a quick tour, showed me the room I would be sleeping in and asked me about my trip.

Do you have a week? I thought. Instead, I smiled and said, "It's been great."

She caught me gazing out the window at the mountains in the distance.

"Do you feel like taking a walk?" she asked.

I looked into her eyes and could sense that she was hoping I'd say "yes", the wedding pressures obviously mounting.

"You probably need to stretch your legs from your drive," she added.

Honestly, my legs were feeling the effect of the miles I had covered earlier, but as I looked out the window, I thought, "It sure would be great to be up there."

We hopped into her car and drove 8 miles up a

gravel mountain road to a trailhead on Sauk Mountain, a peak in the Northern Cascades. The mountain air was remarkably colder. I shivered from the chill. We headed up the narrow trail, stopping occasionally to take a picture as the view unfolded. It was breathtaking.

The river below was surrounded by mountain meadows and evergreens. At one point, I thought, "It would be great to stand in the middle of a mountain meadow," only to realize that at that very moment, I was.

We talked as we negotiated the switchbacks towards the peak—about future plans and the frantic pace that each of our lives had been on for the past several years as she finished her medical residency and I expanded my business. We talked about the dance of relationships and how even some of the best ones have their challenges. We talked about God and His grace in never giving us something that we can't handle.

As the sun set on the mountain, a purple hue was cast on the sky. The clouds moved in like floating cotton. By this time, we were high enough to be staring at them from above. Despite the waning light, we pressed on towards the top, breathing a little faster and feeling the muscles in our legs tightening. One more steep ascent—and we were there.

To say the view was phenomenal is an understatement. We fell silent for a few moments as we gazed at the snow covered rocky peak of Mount Baker. Directly below us was a clear mountain lake. The sun had just set. Each breath I took seemed to fill every cell of my being with clean, crisp air.

And there at the top of a mountain, I heard God say, "I am big enough to take care of you. Take this in and remember Me." We bowed our heads, thankful for the lessons of our life and the opportunity to experience God's presence in the glory of nature.

As we descended in the darkness, my friend completed her last hike as a single woman—and I completed my first as a changed one.

The wedding went without a hitch and as I stood as one of the bridesmaids listening to the sacred, solemn vows of marriage, I was reminded of the depth of the promise I had made 15 years ago. I needed that reminder.

Concrete, WA—the center of the known Universe. The place where God touched my soul. I had asked for answers and I got them—in the form of a solo trip that I am convinced God put on my schedule. A last minute wedding invitation. Airplane companions. The quiet of the Puget Sound and the grandeur of a mountain all to remind me that God really doesn't give us more than we can handle.

And sometimes, He even makes us take a vacation.

Journey Tip #7

Though the path is sometimes rough,
God never gives us more than we can handle.

If He thinks you are a workaholic,
He just might send you on a vacation.

Chapter 8

See It Like Me

"The noblest pleasure is the joy of understanding."
—Leonardo DaVinci

Ladies, I know you will fully understand this next illustration. Have you ever come home (or been home) and actually really answered the question, "How was your day?" If you are anything like me, most of the time the answer is no longer than one or two words. After all, it takes a little bit of warming up for full disclosure. But, if you've ever really honestly answered the question, your monologue probably included some frustrating points in your day—things that seem significant and sometimes insurmountable. And it's the frustrating stuff that gets the attention.

There is nothing like being able to dump things out of your head like that, and when I choose to dump, I do it well—with all the emotion, color, sights, sounds and smells included. I know my husband is often sitting there thinking, *Get to the point already*. By that time, I'm not usually so easily deterred. Dinner can wait. I continue with my storytelling with verve and gusto until, frankly, sometimes I forget what the point is myself. But when I get it all out, I feel great.

That is, until my husband—or anyone else I might have been talking to—solves my problem or dilemma in one fell swoop.

"Well, all you really need to do is…" End of story.

It's a weird place to be in, isn't it? A huge chunk of your day minimized and solved in one sentence. Disturbingly unsatisfying. You might have thought you were looking for an answer to your problems, but when you got it, you realized it wasn't at all what you really wanted.

I once witnessed an interesting illustration on the art of communication. Two people stood back to back and were asked to share with the other what was before them. The conversation stammered forward as one described a tree and an overcast sky, while the other spoke of a wall and a clock.

They were then asked to face each other. I get it, I thought. Any good speaker could catch onto this illustration. As an observer to this exercise, I realized the point. 80% of communication is body language. It is much better to look at someone when you are talking to them, than to be looking away. Yet, as the conversation continued, each person describing to the other what they were staring at, there was still an air of awkwardness. It was at that point, I realized I was wrong.

Then they were asked to look in the same direction. The conversation began to flow. As they stared at a common viewpoint, not only did their words begin to intertwine, but the tension began to fade. Conversation went from what they were observing, to how each was feeling, to topics that had nothing to do with the view before them. Easy. Relaxed. Free.

The point was a good one. In daily communication with others, sometimes the best stance to take is to attempt to see it the way the other person sees it. Seek first to understand.

We long to communicate what is in our head, not necessarily to procure a solution, but to gain understanding. It is validation that our feelings are real—that we matter. After all, if every time you voice your feelings, you get a solution, it sends the message that you must need fixing. And if you need fixing, then you must be broken. Nobody wants to be reminded of how broken we really are. When it boils down to it, what I really want is to know that it's OK to be me.

I think God knew that about human beings when He created them—after all, we were created in His image. He somehow knew that relationships are solidified from a common viewpoint. A place of non-judgment.

My coach once said, "When things get rough and you don't know where to turn or what to say, remember that God is sitting beside you—and He sees it like you see it." In all the time that I had spent with her and all the conversations we had shared, that statement hit the deepest.

If she was right, then that meant when I was frustrated, He felt it. When I was tired at the end of a 12-hour day, He felt it. When I was confused about the next step that I should take in business, He felt it. He felt it, not because He had to—but because He wanted to. He chose to stand beside me and see it the way I did.

That's pretty humbling, isn't it? The God of the Universe has options, after all. In a blink of an eye, He could answer the prayers and fears of His children the world over. He could go about fixing everything. But I think God yearns for something more. I think what He ultimately wants is a relationship with the creation He loves and longs to communicate with him. He would rather be our friend. And we typically don't make friends with a bubble gum machine. You know, put something in—get something out.

That's what makes journeying with Him such a wonderful thing. I think about some of the great men in the Bible—Enoch, Noah and Abraham—stories of individuals who chose to journey on the narrow path and follow where God led. The stories aren't necessarily always filled with wealth and an easy life. In fact, they were often asked to do things that were unconventional and uncomfortable. But it is written of them what I hope one day can be written about me—they *walked with God*. Beside Him. Looking in the same direction. Talking to Him and being understood.

That's all God really wants from us. A relationship. Open. Honest. Filled with understanding. And I think deep down inside—we wouldn't have it any other way.

Journey Tip #8

People often talk to be understood.
Resist the temptation to fix them.

Instead, sit beside them
and look in the *same* direction.
That's what God does with you.

You just might be enlightened by the view.

Chapter 9

Leaning Hard

"You don't raise heroes, you raise sons. And if you treat them like sons, they'll turn out to be heroes, even if it's just in your own eyes."
—Walter Schirra Sr.

I have three sons. That might come as a surprise to some, as only one of them has my name on his birth certificate. The other two joined our family along the journey. Though I didn't get to hold each of them as a child, each of my sons holds a very special place in my heart. I see a bit of myself in each one of them. Sometimes that's good. Sometimes that's bad.

I set aside a time each week to spend alone with them, doing something meaningful—something that I hope they will remember for a lifetime. Some might think I set aside that time because that's what a good mom does. But the secret is I love that part of my journey so much that I would do it anyway. And it is in those times that I've learned some of life's greatest lessons.

This is a story of my number one son. He is called that because he was the first to join our family—he is actually my husband's half brother.

It was the Summer of 1992. I was 24-years old. He was 15. He showed up with an awkwardness that accompanies most adolescent boys. Tall, lanky and not too talkative. When he spoke, it was often in the form of one or two word mumblings and usually only in response to a question. Our conversations used to go something like this:

"Hey, how was school?"

"Good."

"Do you have any homework?"

"No."

"Do you need any help with anything?"

"No."

End of conversation.

We got legal guardianship of him in August—and less than a week later, I found out I was 4 months pregnant. Our family went from two to three to four in less than a year.

We lived in a one-bedroom apartment at the time. His bedroom was a corner of our living room—and that depended on the time of day. He slept on a futon mattress, literally. Just the mattress. It would be rolled out onto the floor by night and be rolled up and out of the way by day. His bedroom also doubled as our dining room and my office. I never once heard him complain about it.

I don't know how it happened, but somewhere along the way, I really began to love this boy. I took him shopping and he convinced me that pants were supposed to be big enough to fit a small family in them. I bought him his first mountain bike, and when that one got stolen, I saved up some money and bought him another one, this time with a chain. We used to ride the trails until we were scarred, sweaty and dusty. I taught him that he needed to wear a helmet—and he showed me why.

I bought him his first pair of rollerblades and taught him how to skate. Well, actually, he taught himself by just taking off down the sidewalk—short, choppy strides, arms flailing. In a matter of a few weeks, he was jumping up onto park benches and skating down steps. I remember the day he proudly showed me how he could skate backwards in the apartment parking lot. He was 15 years old. We used to play roller hockey. I was honored that he invited me to play with his friends. He was grateful, I'm sure, when I scored some impressive goals. We still skate together—every Sunday morning. Our conversations are way better now. It is one of the highlights of my week.

He was the first model in my exercise videos. If he got a bad grade in school, I would ask him to do a whole bunch of exercises so I could have them on film to use in my classroom. He would jump, squat, skip and hop until it was documented to my satisfaction. He wasn't exactly the best student. As a result, I got some good footage—and he got in shape.

He played on his high school basketball team, and I was on the booster club. I cheered for him from the stands, whether they won or lost. I was his biggest fan.

His years in high school flew by. Parent/teacher conferences. Youth group mission trips. Driver's education. His first accident—in my car. Field days. Homecoming.

We finally bought a house at the end of his senior year. It would be the first time he had a room with a door. The minute we signed the papers, he moved his stuff in—a few days before the rest of us did. Before I knew it, he was getting ready to leave for college.

I can remember the day clearly. My husband and I planned on celebrating his departure. The house would seem bigger, the grocery bill smaller. But as I hugged and kissed him goodbye and he jumped in his car to go, I felt something in my heart shift. I sat next to my husband on the porch steps, head in my hands, as my number two son leaned on our backs with his arms around our necks. We were silent until his car disappeared—and then for a few minutes longer. It was anything but a celebration. All of a sudden, I felt old and a little lonely. He was 19 and I was 29.

He came home several times a year after that. And when he did, his schedule was filled with visiting old friends and other social engagements. We mandated a Family Night, one non-negotiable night a week where he would socialize with us, just so we could talk to the boy that was now a man. That tradition still continues to this day, by the way.

My number one son, who came wearing baggy jeans and black t-shirts, now sat at the table with khaki pants, shirt and tie and a copy of the Investors Business Daily. He reads literature—he is a big fan of Winston Churchill. He writes poetry that is heartfelt and beautiful. He is at once a sensitive, caring man and a fun-loving boy.

I would be lying if I made it sound like everything was always wonderful where he was concerned. There were some dark times—some times when I knew for sure I was failing him as a mother and times when I wish he could have perfected the script of the ideal son. There were times he would do things that I did not understand—times when I wanted to just send him home. And there were the darkest times in his life when all I wanted to do was hold him and make his hurt go away. In reality, all I had the power to do was sit and pray for him. There were all those kinds of times. But, when the smoke clears, and I look back on the years since he walked into my life, it's the good stuff I really remember.

He moved back home after graduating from college and began to work for my husband's company. He was responsible for managing the build-out of my second private practice—a job I wouldn't have wished on my worst enemy.

The city building department delayed the project by months on three separate occasions. The management and rescheduling of subcontractors was a logistical nightmare. We ran out of money months before the project was completed and were faced with the daunting task of getting a clinic open on a wing and a prayer while keeping the creditors at bay until we could generate some cash flow. We worked long hours to complete many of the projects ourselves.

It was easily one of the darkest times in my life. After one particularly stressful meeting where our financial picture was discussed, I stood up from the table and said sarcastically, "Well, that was a great way to end the day." And I walked out of the office.

Driving away with tears in my eyes, frustrated and angry at the situation I had gotten myself into, it was my number one son who called my cell phone moments later and left a message saying, "Don't worry. We've made it this far. We are going to get through this. God hasn't let us down yet. Just keep praying." I felt humbled by his faith, stamina and willpower. My boy was now teaching me.

He was 27 and I was 37.

One day he told me he met a girl. "This one is going to be the end of me," he said. I knew the moment he spoke of her that she would probably be the one. For years, I had been prying to find out what kind of girl he actually liked. I knew he had dated other girls before, but in all of the years he was with us, I never got to meet one. "They aren't worthy enough to bring home," he would explain. I guess I should have taken that as a compliment.

In a whirlwind romance that mirrored my own, he described his feelings for her. Feelings of extreme love and devotion—and inadequacy. *I want to be a better man for her,* he wrote to me. In a matter of weeks, the decision was made for her to move from Florida to Michigan.

It's do or die time, he emailed me one day. *I would*

like to know what you think and what the best course of action is. Let me know if you think this is too hasty of a move. I don't, but it's a lot of responsibility on my shoulders. I know that we can do it together and I know she is committed to me and I to her. And then he added one of the most beautiful statements I think I've ever read: *I keep telling her to lean hard on me and I will lean hard on her and together we will stand.*

Leaning hard. That's what it's all about after all, isn't it? A mutual act of depending on the ones you love. An act of equal dependence that makes it OK for even the strongest, most independent person to need someone—because if you don't both lean hard enough, then the whole thing falls over. This overachieving perfectionist needed to hear that. My boy was teaching me again.

He called me the other day while I was at work. "I just wanted to let you know that the wedding date is in a couple of months." It was the day of our family night.

"Wow. Congratulations. Thanks for calling me. Aren't you coming to dinner tonight?" I asked, wondering about the reason for his call.

"Yeah," he replied. "I just wanted you to know before I told everyone else."

He was 28 and I was 38—and in that moment, I felt my heart shift again. I'm not sure he will ever understand how thankful I am that he walked into my life. I feel the nostalgic pangs of someone much older and somehow I don't feel deserving of that.

The journey sometimes brings you lessons from the most unlikely sources. It behooves us to keep our eyes open and stay in the mix. Because sometimes it takes years to realize that the ones we need the most in our lives are the ones we thought only needed us—the kids that grow up to one day become our teachers.

Lean hard.

Journey Tip #9

Lean hard on the ones you love.

When the winds of life howl—
It is what will keep the strong standing.

Chapter 10

Flame and Fragrance

"And we know that all things work together for good
to those who love God,
to those who are the called according to His purpose."
–Romans 8:28 (NKJV)

August 5, 2005. The day I turned 38. I had just finished up a 50-hour workweek and was frantically racing home to change my clothes. In less than an hour, friends, family and the staff of MIHP would convene at MIHP West in Royal Oak, MI for a dedication service. As I maneuvered through the traffic, thoughts of the journey raced through my head.

It was once said that God's will is more easily seen in retrospect. It doesn't always make much sense when you're going through it. After all, if I had planned the journey I would have left out about 90% of the stressful parts. I would have never run out of money or missed a night of sleep. I would have met payroll a week ahead of time every time and never had to work longer than an 8-hour day, and I certainly would not have delayed the process by 9 months.

As I made my way home, I pondered the lessons I was granted along the journey. The people I had met. The team that was built. The lessons in faith and trust. I now know that had the journey gone my way, the foundation of something really special may never have been laid.

"You are the light of the world," the pastor read, as he delivered his dedication message. He lit a candle. "You might do things a little better or a little differently, but the true difference in this clinic is that it has a flame and fragrance all its own." A beacon of light to those who needed hope. And the smell of something different—something unique. A purpose larger than this earth.

As we knelt together in the gym corporately asking the Lord to be with us in this venture, the light and scent of the candle amidst us, I knew I had once again landed in the right place.

In a time when it was viewed as inappropriate to discuss religion in the workplace, my entire team had voluntarily assembled to dedicate this venture to the glory of God.

In a time when productivity often had to be linked to benefits and incentives, I was blessed with a staff driven by a higher purpose—the purpose of something much bigger. Not just healing bodies, but changing lives.

In a time when bosses often failed as leaders, I knew this venture would not fail. Because, though I might stumble as a leader along the way, we were journeying as a team—being led by the greatest Leader of all time.

It was now time for a toast.

"The last time we did this, we were standing in

a different building almost 3 years ago," I said. "I can't believe we're doing it again. Those of you close to me know how difficult this journey was and I have a lot of people to thank. First, to the staff of MIHP…" As I looked each of them in the eye I hoped they felt the depth of my gratitude. I had a story about each one of them that I hold near to my heart.

"I couldn't have done it without you—and frankly, I wouldn't have wanted to," I said. Raising my glass, I completed the toast. "So, here's to the future of MIHP and TriPLAYnar Technology—powered by God."

The staff had one more surprise—my birthday present. As they directed everyone to the lobby, one of them stood and said, "Sherry doesn't just heal our bodies, she heals our souls. I can tell you a million lessons I've learned from the MIHP treatment table." And with that, he unveiled an inscription on the front wall of the lobby:

"Trust only movement.

Life happens at the level of events—not words.

Trust movement."

A testament to moving forward. A testament to practicing what you preach. In a very real sense, they gave me the gift that will keep on giving. Every time I walk through those doors, I will be reminded to keep on keepin' on. Not just for me. But for the team of people who have journeyed with me—poised, willing and able to bring hope to those in need and make a difference in this world.

After all, the journey requires movement, doesn't it? MIHP West—the vehicle that God chose to teach me some of life's greatest lessons. The journey didn't at all go the way that I had planned—and I now knew, I wouldn't have changed a thing.

Journey Tip #10

When you ask God for His will to be done—
Be ready for the unexpected.

He works all things for the good—
To mold you into something that
Shines a little brighter…
And smells a whole lot better.

Chapter 11

Still Waters

"He leads me beside still waters. He restores my soul"
—*Psalm 23:2,3 (NIV)*

There is a place in Southwest Michigan that beckons to the hearts of journeyers. A place where silence and solitude surround the ones who venture onto its grounds. A place where one can go to hear the still, small voice of God in the forest, or fields—or beside still waters.

That's the name of this special place—Still Waters—a silent retreat set on 71-acres in Buchanan, MI. The day I heard about it, I knew I had to go there.

"So let me get this straight," my husband said. "You want to drive three hours and pay to stay at a place where you get to talk to nobody?"

"Exactly," I replied with a dreamy tone in my voice.

It was mid-September. Business had picked up. My teaching semester had begun and the fall seminar season was in full swing. It was the time of year when it seemed all I did was talk.

I arranged to leave town on a Thursday night and be back early Saturday morning. A turbo trip—but I would take whatever I could get.

As I prepared to leave the office, my staff stood around with grins on their faces.

"What?" I asked as I pushed open the door to leave.

"Is there anything you need to say before you go silent?" one said incredulously.

I rolled my eyes and said, "You guys…" Clearly

they didn't get it. Frankly, I'm not sure I did either. But a friend once told me that when you arrive at this place, it is so silent that you realize just how noisy your head is. And if you stay long enough, the voices in your head actually stop.

Really.

I made the trip with a friend, and as we made our way onto the highway, I felt the pressure of a hectic week begin to fade. Several hours later, we turned onto a dark country road and in moments, we were there.

I had no expectations of what I would get out of this trip. I would be thankful if all I got was two nights of uninterrupted sleep. Little did I know the journey would hold far more for me than that.

We made our way through an arched trellis and up a long narrow path to the retreat house. The porch light illuminated our way. I knocked on the door and heard her voice.

"C'mon in!" she said.

The screen door of the house creaked as I opened it. We stepped in and the woman behind the voice came around the corner.

Still Waters is owned and operated by a young couple in their sixties, Delcy and Tom Kuhlman. Tom is in charge of maintaining the property while Delcy serves as the retreat director, cooking meals and offering spiritual guidance to those who request it.

Delcy stood a few inches shorter than me. She has a full head of white hair. She was dressed comfortably, wearing a couple of shirts, some cotton pants and house slippers. And she had an incredible smile. It is the kind of smile that betrays the depth of a woman—one that, in an instant, can warm a room and see right into the depths of your heart.

She showed me around before asking me to choose a room. I chose a small one at the end of the hallway, complete with a bed, desk, nightstand and rocking chair. There was a stuffed animal sitting on top of the comforter.

"This is my favorite room," Delcy said sweetly as she waved me in. "When you turn the lights off, the lights from the parking lot are just bright enough for you to see the giant oak tree just outside the window."

"Thanks. This is great," I said, as I set my backpack on the floor. She gave me a few more instructions about the nature of a silent retreat and the meal schedule and with that, she was gone.

As I settled into my room, I could hear the sound of acorns falling off of the tree outside and the sound of rain hitting the leaves. I could already begin to feel the quieting of my soul.

The next morning, I awoke realizing I had just gotten the first uninterrupted night of sleep I'd had in months. Jumping out of bed, I hurriedly got dressed. After all, I was only going to be here for a day. I had to make the most of it.

After grabbing a quick bite to eat, I headed out for a morning hike. I had seen a map of the grounds and knew there were about three miles of wooded trails surrounding the property. I had arranged to meet with Delcy sometime in the morning and I wanted to be sure to be back in time to take advantage of my only talk time of the day.

Now, if you know anything about me, you would know that it didn't really matter that I saw a map at all. I am horrible at reading them and frankly, I could have had a talking GPS system attached to my belt and still had trouble. I think I looked at the map just as a formality. That's what my husband would tell you anyways.

I set out on a different path three times while I was there. And three times, I got lost. Well, thank God, not totally lost. But, once I thought I was going to end up at the east end of the property, and instead I ended up at the west end right by the entrance gate. I laughed it off and found another path to navigate, only to realize I had walked in a circle twice and landed at somebody else's house three times. I managed to make my way towards the sound of the road and ended up walking a half a mile down a dirt road back to the Still Waters gate.

Lest you think my hiking was all in vain, I'll let you in on the value of getting lost in the woods with all the time in the world at your disposal.

It doesn't really matter.

It was raining lightly the entire time, but due to the heavy tree cover, I didn't get wet. I walked by a tree perch twice and decided to climb it. Now I know what it feels like to be an owl—or at the very least a hunter without a gun. I was only about 15 feet above the ground, but sitting there in the silence of the woods at the level of the tree branches, I somehow felt closer to God.

I walked by a long boardwalk that ended in an isolated lake with—you guessed it—still water. There was an overturned boat at the end of the dock, and I leaned up against it taking in the fresh air. I silently talked to God.

Oh, and the best part about getting lost in the woods—you can sing at the top of your lungs without scaring anyone. And sing I did. I figured if I was here to clear my head, I might as well tune the vocal chords while I was at it. Come to think of it, maybe I did scare someone and that is why I was alone in the woods. At the very least, I figured it would keep the wild animals away.

You know the age-old question. If a tree falls in the forest and nobody is around to hear it, does it still make a sound? Well, I figured the same rule could apply for my singing. If nobody was around to hear it, then I must not be breaking the silent retreat rule. But, I digress.

My poor sense of direction turned a quick morning hike into a 3-hour excursion. I made it back to the retreat house just in time for lunch. I was wet and a little cold, but I hadn't felt this good in a long time. I was disappointed to have missed my time with Delcy, but I figured it probably wasn't meant to be.

"It's not morning anymore," I heard her say as she came around the corner. The look in her eyes and her smile—that smile—all of a sudden made me wish I hadn't missed my time with her.

"Sorry," I said sheepishly, not wanting to explain the reason for my tardiness.

"I have to put lunch on the table and then I am meeting with someone at two-thirty. Would you like to meet with me at four?" she asked. Her perception is incredible, I thought. But even then, I had no idea the depth of the person I had already met.

"Sure," I answered. Maybe it *was* meant to be.

After lunch, I laid on the couch in the living room reading a book I had pulled off of the library shelf. There was a CD player on the shelf beside me and I had taken the liberty to load up some George Winston classics. This is the life, I thought. As my mind pondered the spiritual things I was reading, I felt a sense of clarity and comfort that I realized I had been longing for. As I was on my walk, I had asked God to speak to me—to reveal what I needed to get out of this excursion. I hadn't heard a voice, but I know now that God uses many things to speak to one's soul.

"Sherry, are you ready?" I heard her say. I looked up, surprised that the time had flown so quickly.

"Yeah," I said as I jumped up off of the couch. She led me through the kitchen and down a couple of steps to her study. It was a quaint room, complete with a couch and rocking chair. There were candles on the coffee table; one had a figure of people holding hands surrounding it. The view from the window wall was of the lake at the bottom of the hill.

I sat on the couch and she took her spot on the rocking chair. When I looked up at her, I was met with a gaze that seemed to see right through me. And there was that smile. Unnerving.

"I like to silently pray before I begin talking to someone," she said, "just to invite God into the conversation and ask Him to reveal what we really need to talk about." And with that, we bowed our heads.

I heard her say, "Come Holy Spirit. Amen," and then I looked up. She took a deep breath, leaned back in her rocking chair, crossed her legs and she quietly said, "So, tell me who Sherry is."

"That's a loaded question, " I replied, not really expecting to answer it. I wasn't sure what a spiritual guide did, but I was pretty sure she hadn't signed up to hear about the complications of my life. When I didn't answer, she just continued to smile and stare at me.

Realizing this was when silence would not be appropriate, I took a deep breath and began to speak. "Well, I'm a wife and a mother of an autistic boy," I said, "I own a business and just opened my second private practice." As I listed off the roles I played and the complexity of my daily life, she listened with an empathy unparalleled by anyone I had ever encountered before in my life. I hesitate to tell you the rest of the story, as I swore I would not have more than one chapter in this book where I was crying. But, then again, it is part of the story.

As she reflected back on things I said and validated the feelings of fear and exhaustion that seemed to surround my existence, I felt the tears welling up.

"Does some of that need to come out?" she asked gently. I nodded, looked away and in moments, I was reduced to tears. Now, those of you that know me understand that I am way more likely to get lost than to cry in front of someone. I had walked into her study planning on talking about—well, I don't know exactly what I had planned on talking about. But crying certainly would have never made the agenda.

As I stared out the window, she began to tell me stories from her past. Stories that explained the depth of who she was. It was then I realized that she understood exactly what I was going through.

The conversation continued with her words of counsel. She would occasionally stop to consult her PDA to read a bible verse. I pondered the irony of a woman so simple, surrounded by old-fashion furnishings, being proficient on a PDA. It was a reminder of how timeless her counsel was. Wise beyond her years—yet hip enough to matter. She only got up once to get a wastebasket so I could unload the growing wad of tissues in my lap.

"What does your heart need right now?" she asked.

I stared out the window for a long time before answering. "I just need to know that I'm doing the right thing, walking the right path and being who I need to be for the people that really matter to me. I need to know that everyone is going to be OK."

"But, you realize, God doesn't ask you to be God?" she said. I looked up at her. "It isn't your responsibility to fix anybody or anything. He never asked you to do that. Oh, Sherry, how could he ask you to take on more than you are already handling?" The tears continued to stream down my face. She pulled out her PDA and began to read from Psalm 56.

"You number my wanderings. Put my tears into Your bottle. Are they not in Your book? When I cry out to You, then my enemies will turn back. This I know, because God is for me." She paused to let that sink in. "You know," she continued, "the Hebrews actually had bottles for their tears. And I bet God has a bottle for yours."

I took comfort in her words and all of a sudden felt like it was OK to be where I was, doing what I was doing. As I stared out the window, I saw Tom walk by. Does he have any idea what an incredible woman he married, I thought.

"God isn't a fixer," she said. "If He was, your son wouldn't be the way he is. He never promised that He would fix everything. But what He does promise is that He will never leave us." She paused. "Have you ever read Romans 8:28?" she asked.

I nodded.

"When I was in the seminary, I realized the most accurate translation of that verse from the Greek actually says: "And we know that in all things, God works for the good of those who love Him who have been called according to His purpose," she recited. "He never said all things would be good—but He promised that He would work things out for His children."

I felt layers of walls inside me come down—walls I had no idea I had put up. Her gentle counsel and genuine empathy peeled away layers of hurt and frustration so deep that for the first time in months, I felt at once the most vulnerable I had ever been—and the safest.

"How do you know God is working in your life?" she asked.

"You know, I've seen it," I replied. "And that's what makes this all so frustrating. I've asked Him for signs, and He's delivered. I've stepped out in faith and He has continued to provide. I really hope He understands that my tears come, not because I doubt Him working in my life, but because I am just plain exhausted."

"He knows," she replied softly. And I believed her.

"Come ye who are heavy laden and I will give you rest. Take my yoke upon you and learn from me…" she recited from Matthew 11:28-30. "You've heard that verse before. Did you pick up the 'learn from me' part? Jesus didn't run around trying to fix everyone's stuff when He was on this earth. But He loved everyone. He was gentle and humble—and He remembered to rest in His Father."

I had read that verse countless times before, but that particular phrase had never jumped out at me like it did at that moment. She was right. He never asked me to do more than I could handle—and He wanted me to rest.

"How is it you allow yourself to rest?" she asked.

I laughed at the question. She just stared at me—again, she expected an answer. "I come here," I replied.

"And the last time you were here was…" she said sarcastically.

Ah, intelligent, empathic AND a sense of humor.

"You are the salt of the earth, Delcy," I said as I leaned back. Calm. Grateful. Spent.

"I smell like it sometimes, too," she said humorously.

It had been almost 2 hours since I walked into her study. But before I left, she asked if she could pray with me. My tears had dried up. I didn't think it was possible for me to cry anymore—ever again. She leaned forward, held my hands and prayed a sincere prayer of thanks and hope, and a prayer for rest.

When her prayer ended, I leaned forward to give her a hug. I felt her arms wrap around me, one hand on my back, the other on the back of my head, and there in the quiet of her office as she held me like a child, my tears flowed onto her shoulder. And she didn't let go—for a long time.

If Delcy isn't an angel, then she definitely deserves to be one. I now know that I've been touched by one who walks with God daily, and so closely, that when you talk to her or she holds you or she simply just smiles—you can feel Him. That's why that smile was so unnerving. There is, frankly, nothing like it.

After dinner, I decided to try my hand at navigating the trails one more time. With my newfound clarity, I figured it would be a piece of cake. Wrong. Got lost again. I'm not even going to belabor you with the details except to say that my feet wandered as my mind did. Then, I heard a snort and a deer bolted across my path. That was enough to get this city girl out of the woods—and how. I ended up at the far end of this large field, laughing at my foolish sense of direction and at my fear of the killer deer.

I wandered over to the part of the property where three wooden crosses stood. As I looked over my shoulder, I could see a labyrinth that had been mowed into the grass. In the center of the maze was a large white stone.

Labyrinths have been known to man for 4,000 years and used as a form of walking meditation. Walking the labyrinth was supposed to create a deep awareness of our relationship with ourselves, others and God. What someone chose to do while they walked was as varied as the individuals themselves, but some suggestions were to quiet the mind, ask a question, repeat a phrase or word, read scripture or pray for help.

By this time, I welcomed the opportunity to walk without the added stress of having to navigate, so I stepped into the labyrinth. As I walked, I found myself gazing ahead, trying to figure out how close I was to the end of it. Several times, I thought I my next turn would land me in the center of the maze, only to have the path redirect me to another part of the circle.

I had to laugh as the point of my wanderings became clear. It was as if God was saying, "It isn't your job to know the end of the journey. It is your job to step out in faith, take it one step at a time and follow the path I give you." I had set out on several paths that day with my own map in mind. You already know how far that got me. Now it was time for me to give up the driver's seat to the One who never got lost.

As this lesson became clear, I found myself able to free my mind of distractions. My thoughts went back to my meeting with Delcy, as phrases from our conversation reverberated through my head.

"God isn't a fixer."

"Take my yoke upon you and learn from Me."

"God never asked you to be God."

"I bet God has a bottle for your tears."

"He promised that He would never leave you."

As the path of the maze led me, I was able to clear my mind. By the time I reached the center of the labyrinth, I had made peace with myself and God. I sat on the rock, and bowed my head in a silent prayer of thanks for the experiences of the day. I felt the warmth of the sun on my face and could see the light penetrating through my closed eyes. I looked up just in time to see the sun setting behind the three wooden crosses.

The evening could have ended there to my total satisfaction, but I felt compelled to continue my walk. I walked the labyrinth out and headed down the hill towards the lake. I wanted to sit beside still waters one more time. As I sat and recited Psalm 23, I realized at that moment how completely satisfied my soul was. I really wasn't wanting for anything. The voices in my head had stopped hours ago. No worries. No rush. Pure rest.

I headed up the hill to my final stop of the night—the large swing hanging from the branch of the oak tree that was just outside my room. As I sat on the swing, I realized it was set just high enough so my feet barely touched the ground. I felt like a child just waiting for someone to come by and give me a push. As I leaned back and looked up, I saw the moon, full and bright, rising gently to its place in the sky, framed by the large branches of the oak tree.

I must have sat there for an hour, captivated by the view before me. The reflection of the trees on the still water of the lake was so clear, I swore the trees were growing upside down. The cool night air coupled with the strong silence of Still Waters served as the perfect ending to a perfect day.

Eventually, I went inside. As I packed my things in preparation for my very early departure the next morning, I wished only to be able to say goodbye to Delcy—to the one who had reached in and touched my heart.

I heard a knock on the door. My friend told me Delcy was waiting for me in the living room. As I walked out to meet her, she stood in the middle of the room smiling at me with her arms open. I leaned over and accepted her embrace.

"I'm so sorry you have to leave so soon," she quietly whispered in my ear. I know she said it for my benefit, but I was half hoping it would mean that she would miss me too.

"Don't worry," I replied. "I will be back."

As we drove away from Still Waters early the next morning, the lessons from my journey ran through my head. I had anticipated getting some sleep—and I was given so much more.

God never said He would fix everything in my life. But He promised in all things He would work for the good of those who loved Him. He promised He would never leave us. And He promised if we came to Him weary—He would give us rest.

Thank God He keeps His promises.

Journey Tip #11

God isn't a fixer.

He never promised only good things would come to His children.

But He did promise He would never leave us.

And He promised He would work all things (even the bad stuff) for the good.

He also promised that if we get tired, He would give us rest.

And God always keeps His promises.

Chapter 12

Finishing Well

"I have fought the good fight, I have finished the course,
I have kept the faith."
—2 Timothy 4:7 (ASV)

The thing about journeying is this—there are times when you must turn right, veer left or go straight ahead. There are times when you run and times when it seems like you are moving in slow motion. And then there are those times when you just stop to look back at where you have been.

It had been over 8 months since I had started seeing my coach. The timing of our initial meeting could not have been any better. I had come through one of the toughest seasons of my life. At times I felt like I resembled someone who had been put through a washer cycle— agitated, rinsed and spun dry. The good news is, I felt stronger and healthier—more like who I was meant to be. One can handle the agitation if it cleans all of the mud out of your system.

The inevitable end to our meetings seemed just around the corner. Though I drew comfort from our weekly sessions, it had become apparent to me that our job in that particular space was near completion.

"This is definitely a nice to do thing for me now," I said. "Not a need to do thing."

She smiled and said, "I'm glad you brought that up. I have been saving this conversation in my back pocket for just the right time."

I smiled at her intuition.

"There's nothing wrong with realizing that a season of your life has ended. You have learned so many things. Every life has seasons…and seasons change. I see a lot of people who come in here, and then just decide to stop coming for no reason. There are those that just sort of disappear and I have no idea what happened to them. Then there are the ones who just keep on coming…" she explained. "You have done the work. You are strong and healthy. When you walk with God and honor His will, there is usually something to celebrate," she said. She paused to let that sink in before she added, "There's something to be said for finishing well."

Students of literature classify dramas as either comedies or tragedies. The difference has very little to do with humor. In fact, what makes a comedy is that the narrative moves from conflict toward reconciliation and resolution, while a tragedy ends with a catastrophe. Shakespeare's tragedies usually end with a death scene— the comedies end in a wedding.

The point is that even comedies have conflict. It is our human nature to despair at the first signs of it. The story of our lives often feels like its headed towards a tragedy. But though it may seem like there is no reason for optimism, there is always a reason for hope.

"Optimism is a matter of optics, of seeing what you want to see
and not seeing what you don't want to see.
Hope, on the other hand, is a Christian virtue.
It is the unblinking acknowledgment
of all that militates against hope,
and the unrelenting refusal to despair."
—Richard John Neuhaus

When one chooses to walk with God, one really has no reason—or right—to despair. That is the biggest lesson I will take away from this season of my journey. Because no matter how tumultuous things might get, the author and finisher of my faith has it written like a comedy. There may be conflict and tears, but there will also be laughs—and the Good Book says, it ends with a wedding.

I smiled at my coach, knowing my time with her had been well spent. The lessons I learned during the toughest season of my life will stay with me long after I walk out of her office for the last time.

The bumps and bruises one gets while traveling on a narrow mountain trail seem inconsequential once you make it to the top and can appreciate the view. At 30,000 feet, the sun feels a little bit warmer and things always look a little bit different.

Even as I write this, it is late October in Michigan. It is a cool, fall day, and as I look out the window, I realize I am surrounded by the most brilliant display of color. Yellow. Red. Orange. Creation bursting in final celebration of yet another season completed. Absolutely breathtaking.

I smiled at the irony.

There is, after all, something to be said about finishing well.

Journey Tip #12

See the journey all the way through.
When you journey with the Lord,
What seems like a tragedy
controlled by the world,
Is really a comedy—authored by God.

Live in that hope…and finish well.

Visit us on-line at:
www.lessonsfromthejourney.com

Appendix
(Tools for the Journey...and other stuff)

Dangerous Woman

*"…the opposite of a nice girl is a dangerous woman.
A woman who shows up with everything she is and joins the battle
against whatever opposes the redeeming work of God
in our lives and in our world."*
–Lynne Hybels

Every now and then, you come across a book that speaks volumes to your soul. Sometimes you come across them in bookstores. Or you might get one as a gift. And sometimes, they even get delivered by angels themselves.

Human angels, that is. The people that walk into your life and touch you in a way that you needed to be touched—at just the right time.

I got such a delivery one day. It was towards the end of another hectic week and I was just winding up a staff meeting when someone dropped it off at the front desk and promptly whisked out the door. It came with a card filled with words of affirmation and the title of the book immediately made me smile: <u>Nice Girls Don't Change the World</u>. Nice girls might not change the world, but good, God-fearing women do.

Here is one of my favorite quotes from the book:

A good woman's life is grounded in the word of God.
A good woman's knows her unique life matters to God.
A good woman doesn't let fear stop her.
A good woman is a dangerous woman.

"You have an answer to the world's needs
that is yours alone."

Thank you, Susie Vanker, for thinking of me—and for being a human angel in my life.

RISKS

To laugh is to risk appearing the fool.

To weep is to risk appearing sentimental.

To reach out for another is to risk involvement.

To expose feelings is to risk exposing your true self.

To place your ideas, your dreams,

before a crowd is to risk their loss.

To love is to risk not being loved in return.

To live is to risk dying. To hope is to risk failure.

But risk must be taken,

Because the greatest hazard in life is to risk nothing.

If you risk nothing and do nothing, you dull your spirit.

You may avoid suffering and sorrow,

But you cannot learn, feel, change, grow, love and live.

Chained by your attitude, you are a slave.

You have forfeited your freedom.

Only a person who risks is free.

—Author Unknown

Footprints with a Twist

Imagine you and the Lord walking down the road together. For much of the way, the Lord's footprints go along steadily, consistently, rarely varying the pace. But your footprints are a disorganized stream of zigzags, starts, stops, turnarounds, circles, departures and returns. For much of the way, it seems to go on like this, but gradually, your footprints come more inline with the Lord's, soon paralleling His consistently. You and Jesus are walking like true friends.

This seems perfect, but then an interesting thing happens: your footprints, once etched in the sand next to Jesus', are now walking precisely in His steps. Inside His larger footprints are your smaller ones. Safely, you and Jesus are becoming one.

This goes on for many miles, but gradually you notice another change. The footprints inside the larger footprints seem to grow larger. Eventually they disappear altogether. There is only one set of footprints: the two have become one. This goes on for a long time, but suddenly the second set of footprints is back.

This time it seems even worse! Zigzags all over the place. Stops. Starts. Deep gashes in the sand. A veritable mess of prints. You are amazed and shocked.

Your dream ends.

Now you pray:

"Lord, I understand the first scene with zigzags and fits. I was a new Christian: I was just learning. But you walked on through the storm and helped me learn to walk with you."

"That is correct."

"And when the smaller footprints were inside Yours, I was actually learning to walk in your steps; I followed you closely."

"Very good. You have understood everything so far."

"When the smaller footprints grew and filled Yours, I suppose that I was becoming like you in every way."

"Precisely."

"So, Lord, was there a regression or something? The footprints separated, and this time were worse than the first."

There was a pause as the Lord answered with a smile in His voice. *"You didn't know? That was when we danced."*

To everything, there is a season, a time for every purpose under heaven:

A time to weep,
A time to laugh:
A time to mourn,
And a time to dance...

Voice of Truth

(A song by Casting Crowns with my favorite parts bolded)

Oh what I would do to have the kind of faith it takes
To climb out of this boat I'm in, onto the crashing waves.

To step out of my comfort zone into the realm of the unknown where Jesus is. And He's holding out His hand.

But the waves are calling out my name
and they laugh at me.
Reminding me of all the times I've tried before and failed
The waves they keep on telling me time and time again
"Boy, you'll never win!"
"You'll never win!"

Chorus:
But the Voice of Truth tells me a different story
The Voice of Truth says, "Do not be afraid!"
And the Voice of Truth says, "This is for My glory"
Out of all the voices calling out to me
I will choose to listen and believe the Voice of Truth

Oh what I would do to have the kind of strength it takes
to stand before a giant with just a sling and a stone.

Surrounded by the sound of a thousand warriors shaking
in their armor, wishing they'd have had the strength to
stand.

But the giant's calling out my name and he laughs at me.
Reminding me of all the times I've tried before and failed
The giant keeps on telling me time and time again,
"Boy you'll never win!"
"You'll never win!"

But the stone was just the right size
to put the giant on the ground.
And the waves they don't seem so high
on top of them lookin' down.
I will soar with the wings of eagles when I stop
and listen to the sound of Jesus singing over me.

Word Of God Speak
(A song by Mercy Me)

I'm finding myself at a loss for words
And the funny thing is it's okay
The last thing I need is to be heard
But to hear what You would say

Word of God speak
Would You pour down like rain
Washing my eyes to see
Your majesty
To be still and know
That You're in this place
Please let me stay and rest
In Your holiness
Word of God speak

I'm finding myself in the midst of You
Beyond the music, beyond the noise
All that I need is to be with You
And in the quiet hear Your voice

I'm finding myself at a loss for words
And the funny thing is it's okay

Our Thinking vs. **God's Promises**

It is impossible.
All things are possible. (Luke 18:27)

I'm too tired.
I will give you rest! (Matthew 11:28-30)

Nobody really loves me.
I love you. (John 3:16)

I cannot go on.
My grace is sufficient for you. (II Corinthians 12:9)

It is not worth it.
It will be worth it. (Romans 8:28)

I am not able.
I am able. (Romans 8:25)

I can't forgive myself.
I forgive you. (I John 1:9; Romans 8:1)

I can't manage.
I will supply your need. (Philippians 4:19)

I am afraid.
I have not given you a spirit of fear. (II Timothy 1:7)

I am worried.
Cast all your cares on me. (I Peter 5:7)

I have no faith.
**I have given everyone a measure of faith.
(Romans 12:3)**

I am not smart enough.
I give you wisdom. (I Corinthians 1:30)

I feel so alone.
I will never leave you or forsake you. (Hebrews 13:5)

*Talent is God-given. Be thankful.
Fame is man-given. Be humble.
Conceit is self-given. Be careful.*

*When a man is wrapped up in himself, he makes a pretty small
package.*

REALITY...

(An excerpt from a high school speech by Bill Gates)

11 Rules You Did Not and Will Not Learn in School

Rule 1: Life is not fair...get used to it.

Rule 2: The world will not care about your self-esteem. The world will expect you to accomplish something BEFORE you feel good about yourself.

Rule 3: You will NOT make $50,000 a year right out of high school. You won't be a vice-president with a car phone until you earn both.

Rule 4: If you think your teacher is tough...wait till you get a boss.

Rule 5: Flipping burgers are not beneath your dignity. Your grandparents had a different word for burger flipping— they called it opportunity.

Rule 6: If you mess up, it's not your parents' fault, so don't whine about your mistakes, learn from them!

Rule 7: Before you were born, your parents were not as boring as they are now. They got that way from paying your bills, cleaning your clothes and listening to you talk about how cool you are. So before you save the rainforest from the parasites of your parents' generation, try delousing the closet in your own room.

Rule 8: Your school may have done away with winners and losers...but life has not! In some schools, they have abolished failing grades and they'll give you as many times as you want to get the right answer: This doesn't bear the slightest resemblance to ANYTHING in real life.

Rule 9: Life is not divided into semesters. You don't get summers off and very few employers are interested in helping you find yourself. Do that on your own time.

Rule 10: Television is NOT real life. In real life, people actually have to leave the coffee shop and to jobs.

Rule 11: Be nice to nerds. Chances are you'll end up working for one.

God Bless America,

Bill Gates

McLaughlin/Lander Publishing
A Division of
TriPLAYnar Technology, Inc.

Real People. Real Stories. Real Life.

Quick Order Form

Fax Orders: (586) 268-6948. Send this form.

Telephone Orders: (586) 268-6942. Have your credit card ready.

On-line Orders: www.lessonsfromthejourney.com

Postal Orders: ML Publishing
31500 Dequindre Rd.
Warren, MI 48092

Please send me more FREE information on:
Other books   Speaking/Seminars

Name:____
Address:____
City:___________________________State:____Zip:____________
Telephone:____
Email:____

Sales tax: Please add 6% for products shipped to MI addresses.

Shipping by air:
U.S.: $4.00 for first book and $2.00 for each additional product.
International: $9.00 for first book; $5.00 for each additional
product (estimate).

Payment: Check   Credit Card
Visa   Mastercard   AMEX
Card number:____
Name on Card:___________________________Exp. Date:________